C000263051

Carol Ann Duffy was Poet Laureate of the United Kingdom for a decade from 2009 to 2019. Her poetry has received many awards, including the Signal Prize for Children's Verse, the Whitbread, Forward and T. S. Eliot Prizes, and the Lannan and E. M. Forster Awards in America. She won the PEN Pinter Prize in 2012, and was appointed DBE in 2015. In 2021, she was awarded the International Golden Wreath for lifetime achievement in poetry.

Also by Carol Ann Duffy in Picador

Standing Female Nude

Selling Manhattan

The Other Country

Mean Time

The World's Wife

Feminine Gospels

New Selected Poems

Rapture

Mrs Scrooge

Love Poems

Another Night
Before Christmas

The Bees

The Christmas Truce

Wenceslas

Bethlehem

Ritual Lighting

Dorothy Wordsworth's
Christmas Birthday

Collected Poems

The Wren-Boys

The King of
Christmas

Pablo Picasso's Noël

Frost Fair

Sincerity

Christmas Poems

Advent Street

Nature

Elegies

Politics

AS EDITOR

Hand in Hand

Answering Back

To the Moon

Off the Shelf

Empty Nest

LOVE

Carol Ann Duffy

PICADOR

First published 2023 by Picador
an imprint of Pan Macmillan
The Smithson, 6 Briset Street, London EC1M 5NR
EU representative: Macmillan Publishers Ireland Ltd, 1st Floor,
The Liffey Trust Centre, 117–126 Sheriff Street Upper,
Dublin 1, D01 YC43
Associated companies throughout the world
www.panmacmillan.com

ISBN 978-1-5290-9697-2

1 3 5 7 9 8 6 4 2

A CIP catalogue record for this book is available from the British Library.

Printed and bound by CPI Group (UK) Ltd, Croydon, CR0 4YY

Contents

LOVE

Oppenheim's Cup and Saucer

She asked me to luncheon in fur. Far from
the loud laughter of men, our secret life stirred.

I remember her eyes, the slim rope of her spine.
This is your cup, she whispered, and this mine.

We drank the sweet hot liquid and talked dirty.
As she undressed me, her breasts were a mirror

and there were mirrors in the bed. She said Place
your legs around my neck, that's right. Yes.

1985

Lovebirds

I wait for your step.
A jay on the cherry tree
trembles the blossom.

I name you *my love*
and the gulls fly above us
calling to the air.

Our two pale bodies
move in the late light, slowly
as doves do, breathing.

And then you are gone.
A night-owl mourns in darkness
for the moon's last phase.

1985

Warming Her Pearls

Next to my own skin, her pearls. My mistress
bids me wear them, warm them, until evening
when I'll brush her hair. At six, I place them
round her cool, white throat. All day I think of her,

resting in the Yellow Room, contemplating silk
or taffeta, which gown tonight? She fans herself
whilst I work willingly, my slow heat entering
each pearl. Slack on my neck, her rope.

She's beautiful. I dream about her
in my attic bed; picture her dancing
with tall men, puzzled by my faint, persistent scent
beneath her French perfume, her milky stones.

I dust her shoulders with a rabbit's foot,
watch the soft blush seep through her skin
like an indolent sigh. In her looking-glass
my red lips part as though I want to speak.

Full moon. Her carriage brings her home. I see
her every movement in my head . . . Undressing,
taking off her jewels, her slim hand reaching
for the case, slipping naked into bed, the way

she always does . . . And I lie here awake,
knowing the pearls are cooling even now
in the room where my mistress sleeps. All night
I feel their absence and I burn.

1987

Two Small Poems of Desire

1

The little sounds I make against your skin
don't mean anything. They make me
an animal learning vowels; not that I know
I do this, but I hear them
floating away over your shoulders, sticking
to the ceiling. *Aa Ee Iy Oh Uu.*

Are they sounds of surprise
at the strange ghosts your nakedness makes
moving above me in how much light
a net can catch?

Who cares. Sometimes language virtuously used
is language badly used. It's tough
and difficult and true to say
I love you when you do these things to me.

2

The way I prefer to play you back
is naked in the cool lawn of those green sheets,
just afterwards,
and saying *What secret am I?*

I am brought up sharp in a busy street,
staring inwards as you put down your drink
and touch me again. *How does it feel?*

It feels like tiny gardens
growing in the palms of the hands,
invisible,
sweet, if they had a scent.

1990

Girlfriends

derived from Verlaine

That hot September night, we slept in a single bed,
naked, and on our frail bodies the sweat
cooled and renewed itself. I reached out my arms
and you, hands on my breasts, kissed me. Evening of
amber.

Our nightgowns lay on the floor where you fell to your
knees
and became ferocious, pressed your head to my stomach,
your mouth to the red gold, the pink shadows; except
I did not see it like this at the time, but arched

my back and squeezed water from the sultry air
with my fists. Also I remember hearing, clearly
but distantly, a siren some streets away – *de*

da de da de da – which mingled with my own
absurd cries, so that I looked up, even then,
to see my fingers counting themselves, dancing.

1990

Words, Wide Night

Somewhere on the other side of this wide night
and the distance between us, I am thinking of you.
The room is turning slowly away from the moon.

This is pleasurable. Or shall I cross that out and say
it is sad? In one of the tenses I singing
an impossible song of desire that you cannot hear.

La lala la. See? I close my eyes and imagine
the dark hills I would have to cross
to reach you. For I am in love with you and this

is what it is like or what it is like in words.

1990

Who Loves You

I worry about you travelling in those mystical machines.
Every day people fall from the clouds, dead.
Breathe in and out and in and out easy.
Safety, safely, safe home.

Your photograph is in the fridge, smiles when the light
    comes on.
All the time people are burnt in the public places.
Rest where the cool trees drop to a gentle shade.
Safety, safely, safe home.

Don't lie down on the sands where the hole in the sky is.
Too many people being gnawed to shreds.
Send me your voice however it comes across oceans.
Safety, safely, safe home.

The loveless men and homeless boys are out there and
    angry.
Nightly people end their lives in the shortcut.
Walk in the light, steadily hurry towards me.
Safety, safely, safe home. (Who loves you?)
Safety, safely, safe home.

1990

Crush

The older she gets,
the more she awakes
with somebody's face strewn in her head
like petals which once made a flower.

What everyone does
is sit by a desk
and stare at the view, till the time
where they live reappears. Mostly in words.

Imagine a girl
turning to see
love stand by a window, taller,
clever, anointed with sudden light.

Yes, like an angel then,
to be truthful now.
At first a secret, erotic, mute;
today a language she cannot recall.

And we're all owed joy,
sooner or later.
The trick's to remember whenever
it was, or to see it coming.

1993

Adultery

Wear dark glasses in the rain.
Regard what was unhurt
as though through a bruise.
Guilt. A sick, green tint.

New gloves, money tucked in the palms,
the handshake crackles. Hands
can do many things. Phone.
Open the wine. Wash themselves. Now

you are naked under your clothes all day,
slim with deceit. Only the once
brings you alone to your knees,
miming, more, more, older and sadder,

creative. Suck a lie with a hole in it
on the way home from a lethal, thrilling night
up against a wall, faster. Language
unpeels to a lost cry. You're a bastard.

Do it do it do it. Sweet darkness
in the afternoon; a voice in your ear
telling you how you are wanted,
which way, now. A telltale clock

wiping the hours from its face, your face
on a white sheet, gasping, radiant, yes.
Pay for it in cash, fiction, cab-fares back
to the life which crumbles like a wedding-cake.

Paranoia for lunch; too much
to drink, as a hand on your thigh
tilts the restaurant. You know all about love,
don't you. Turn on your beautiful eyes

for a stranger who's dynamite in bed, again
and again; a slow replay in the kitchen
where the slicing of innocent onions
scalds you to tears. Then, selfish autobiographical sleep

in a marital bed, the tarnished spoon of your body
stirring betrayal, your heart over-ripe at the core.
You're an expert, darling; your flowers
dumb and explicit on nobody's birthday.

So write the script – illness and debt,
a ring thrown away in a garden
no moon can heal, your own words
commuting to bile in your mouth, terror –

and all for the same thing twice. And all
for the same thing twice. You did it.
What. Didn't you. Fuck. Fuck. No. That was
the wrong verb. This is only an abstract noun.

1993

Mean Time

The clocks slid back an hour
and stole light from my life
as I walked through the wrong part of town,
mourning our love.

And, of course, unmendable rain
fell to the bleak streets
where I felt my heart gnaw
at all our mistakes.

If the darkening sky could lift
more than one hour from this day
there are words I would never have said
nor have heard you say.

But we will be dead, as we know,
beyond all light.
These are the shortened days
and the endless nights.

1993

Mrs Beast

These myths going round, these legends, fairytales,
I'll put them straight; so when you stare
into my face – Helen's face, Cleopatra's,
Queen of Sheba's, Juliet's – then, deeper,
gaze into my eyes – Nefertiti's, Mona Lisa's,
Garbo's eyes – think again. The Little Mermaid slit
her shining, silver tail in two, rubbed salt
into that stinking wound, got up and walked,
in agony, in fishnet tights, stood up and smiled, waltzed,
all for a Prince, a pretty boy, a charming one
who'd dump her in the end, chuck her, throw her
    overboard.
I could have told her – look, love, I should know,
they're bastards when they're Princes.
What you want to do is find yourself a Beast. The sex

is better. Myself, I came to the House of the Beast
no longer a girl, knowing my own mind,
my own gold stashed in the bank,
my own black horse at the gates
ready to carry me off at one wrong word,
one false move, one dirty look.
But the Beast fell to his knees at the door
to kiss my glove with his mongrel lips – good –
showed by the tears in his bloodshot eyes
that he knew he was blessed – better –
didn't try to conceal his erection,
size of a mule's – best. And the Beast
watched me open, decant and quaff
a bottle of Château Margaux '54,
the year of my birth, before he lifted a paw.

I'll tell you more. Stripped of his muslin shirt
and his corduroys, he steamed in his pelt,
ugly as sin. He had the grunts, the groans, the yelps,
the breath of a goat. I had the language, girls.
The lady says Do this. Harder. The lady says
Do that. Faster. The lady says That's not where I meant.
At last it all made sense. The pig in my bed
was *invited*. And if his snout and trotters fouled
my damask sheets, why, then, he'd wash them. Twice.
Meantime, here was his horrid leather tongue
to scour in between my toes. Here
were his hooked and yellowy claws to pick my nose,
if I wanted that. Or to scratch my back
till it bled. Here was his bullock's head
to sing off-key all night where I couldn't hear.
Here was a bit of him like a horse, a ram,
an ape, a wolf, a dog, a donkey, dragon, dinosaur.

Need I say more? On my Poker nights, the Beast
kept out of sight. We were a hard school, tough as fuck,
all of us beautiful and rich – the Woman
who Married a Minotaur, Goldilocks, the Bride
of the Bearded Lesbian, Frau Yellow Dwarf, et Moi.
I watched those wonderful women shuffle and deal –
Five and Seven Card Stud, Sidewinder, Hold 'Em,
    Draw –

I watched them bet and raise and call. One night,
a head-to-head between Frau Yellow Dwarf and
    Bearded's Bride
was over the biggest pot I'd seen in my puff.
The Frau had the Queen of Clubs on the baize
and Bearded the Queen of Spades. Final card. Queen
    each.
Frau Yellow raised. Bearded raised. Goldilocks' eyes
were glued to the pot as though porridge bubbled there.
The Minotaur's wife lit a stinking cheroot. Me,
I noticed the Frau's hand shook as she placed her chips.

Bearded raised her a final time, then stared,
stared so hard you felt your dress would melt
if she blinked. I held my breath. Frau Yellow
swallowed hard, then called. Sure enough, Bearded flipped
her Aces over; diamonds, hearts, the pubic Ace of Spades.
And that was a lesson learnt by all of us –
the drop-dead gorgeous Bride of the Bearded Lesbian
    didn't bluff.

But behind each player stood a line of ghosts
unable to win. Eve. Ashputtel. Marilyn Monroe.
Rapunzel slashing wildly at her hair.
Bessie Smith unloved and down and out.
Bluebeard's wives, Henry VIII's, Snow White
cursing the day she left the seven dwarfs, Diana,
Princess of Wales. The sheepish Beast came in
with a tray of schnapps at the end of the game
and we stood for the toast – *Fay Wray* –
then tossed our fiery drinks to the back of our crimson
    throats.
Bad girls. Serious ladies. Mourning our dead.

So I was hard on the Beast, win or lose,
when I got upstairs, those tragic girls in my head,
turfing him out of bed; standing alone
on the balcony, the night so cold I could taste the stars
on the tip of my tongue. And I made a prayer –
thumbing my pearls, the tears of Mary, one by one,
like a rosary – words for the lost, the captive beautiful,
the wives, those less fortunate than we.
The moon was a hand-mirror breathed on by a Queen.
My breath was a chiffon scarf for an elegant ghost.
I turned to go back inside. Bring me the Beast for the night.
Bring me the wine-cellar key. Let the less-loving one be me.

1999

White Writing

No vows written to wed you,
I write them white,
my lips on yours,
light in the soft hours of our married years.

No prayers written to bless you,
I write them white,
your soul a flame,
bright in the window of your maiden name.

No laws written to guard you,
I write them white,
your hand in mine,
palm against palm, lifeline, heartline.

No rules written to guide you,
I write them white,
words on the wind,
traced with a stick where we walk on the sand.

No news written to tell you,
I write it white,
foam on a wave
as we lift up our skirts in the sea, wade,

see last gold sun behind clouds,
inked water in moonlight.
No poems written to praise you,
I write them white.

2002

Grace

Then, like a sudden, easy birth, grace –
rendered as light to the softening earth,
the moon stepping slowly backwards
out of the morning sky, reward
for the dark hours we took to arrive and kneel
at the silver river's edge near the heron priest,
anointed, given – what we would wish ourselves.

2005

River

Down by the river, under the trees, love waits for me
to walk from the journeying years of my time and arrive.
I part the leaves and they toss me a blessing of rain.

The river stirs and turns, consoling and fondling itself
with watery hands, its clear limbs parting and closing.
Grey as a secret, the heron bows its head on the bank.

I drop my past on the grass and open my arms, which
ache
as though they held up this heavy sky, or had pressed
against window glass all night as my eyes sieved the stars;

open my mouth, wordless at last meeting love at last, dry
from travelling so long, shy of a prayer. You step from
the shade,
and I feel love come to my arms and cover my mouth, feel

my soul swoop and ease itself into my skin, like a bird
threading a river. Then I can look love full in the face, see
who you are I have come this far to find, the love of my
life.

2005

Absence

Then the birds stitching the dawn with their song
have patterned your name.

Then the green bowl of the garden filling with light
is your gaze.

Then the lawn lengthening and warming itself
is your skin.

Then a cloud disclosing itself overhead
is your opening hand.

Then the first seven bells from the church
pine on the air.

Then the sun's soft bite on my face
is your mouth.

Then a bee in a rose is your fingertip
touching me here.

Then the trees bending and meshing their leaves
are what we would do.

Then my steps to the river are text to a prayer
printing the ground.

Then the river searching its bank for your shape
is desire.

Then a fish nuzzling the water's throat
has a lover's ease.

Then a shawl of sunlight dropped in the grass
is a garment discarded.

Then a sudden scatter of summer rain
is your tongue.

Then a butterfly paused on a trembling leaf
is your breath.

Then the gauzy mist relaxed on the ground
is your pose.

Then the fruit from the cherry tree falling on grass
is your kiss, your kiss.

Then the day's hours are theatres of air
where I watch you entranced.

Then the sun's light going down from the sky
is the length of your back.

Then the evening bells over the rooftops
are lovers' vows.

Then the river staring up, lovesick for the moon,
is my long night.

Then the stars between us are love
urging its light.

2005

The Lovers

Pity the lovers,
who climb to the high room,
where the bed,
and the gentle lamps wait,
and disembark from their lives.
The deep waves of the night
lap at the window.

Time slips away
like land from a ship.
The moon, their own death,
follows them, cold,
cold in their blankets.
Pity the lovers, homeless,
with no country to sail to.

2005

New Year

I drop the dying year behind me like a shawl
and let it fall. The urgent fireworks fling themselves
against the night, flowers of desire, love's fervency.
Out of the space around me, standing here, I shape
your absent body against mine. You touch me as the
giving air.

Most far, most near, your arms are darkness, holding me,
so I lean back, lip-read the heavens talking on in light,
syllabic stars. I see, at last, they pray at us. Your breath
is midnight's, living, on my skin, across the miles
between us,
fields and motorways and towns, the million lit-up little
homes.

This love we have, grief in reverse, full rhyme, wrong place,
wrong time, sweet work for hands, the heart's vocation, flares
to guide the new year in, the days and nights far out upon
the sky's
dark sea. Your mouth is snow now on my lips, cool, intimate,
first kiss,
a vow. Time falls and falls through endless space, to when
we are.

2005

Whatever

I'll take your hand, the left,
and ask that it still have life
to hold my hand, the right,
as I walk alone where we walked,
or to lie all night on my breast,
at rest, or to stop all talk with a finger
pressed to my lips.

I'll take your lips,
ask, when I close my eyes, as though
in prayer, that they ripen out of the air
to be there again on mine,
or to say my name, or to smile, or to kiss
the sleep from my eyes. I'll take

your eyes,
nothing like, lovelier under, the sun,
and ask that they wake to see, to look
at me, even to cry, so long as I feel their tears
on your face, warm rain on a rose.

Your face I'll take, asleep, ask that I learn,
by heart, the tilt of your nose; or awake, and ask
that I touch with my tongue the soft buds of the lobes
of your ears

and I'll take them, too,
ask that they feel my breath shape
into living words, that they hear.

I'll take your breath
and ask that it comes and goes, comes and goes, forever,

like the blush under your cheek, and I'll even settle for
that. Whatever.

2005

Betrothal

I will be yours, be yours.
I'll walk on the moors
with my spade.
Make me your bride.

I will be brave, be brave.
I'll dig my own grave
and lie down.
Make me your own.

I will be good, be good.
I'll sleep in my blankets of mud
till you kneel above.
Make me your love.

I'll stay forever, forever.
I'll wade in the river,
wearing my gown of stone.
Make me the one.

I will obey, obey.
I'll float far away,
gargling my vows.
Make me your spouse.

I will say yes, say yes.
I'll sprawl in my dress
on my watery bed.
Make me be wed.

I'll wear your ring, your ring.
I'll dance and I'll sing
in the flames.
Make me your name.

I'll feel desire, desire.
I'll bloom in the fire.
I'll blush like a baby.
Make me your lady.

I'll say I do, I do.
I'll be ash in a jar, for you
to scatter my life.
Make me your wife.

2005

Art

Only art now – our bodies, brushstroke, pigment, motif;
our story, figment, suspension of disbelief;
the thrum of our blood, percussion;
chords, minor, for the music of our grief.

Art, the chiselled, chilling marble of our kiss;
locked into soundless stone, our promises,
or fizzled into poems; page print
for the dried flowers of our voice.

No choice for love but art's long illness, death,
huge theatres for the echoes that we left,
applause, then utter dark;
grand opera for the passion of our breath;

and the Oscar-winning movie in your heart;
and where my soul sang, croaking art.

2005

Echo

I think I was searching for treasures or stones
in the clearest of pools
when your face . . .

when your face,
like the moon in a well
where I might wish . . .

might well wish
for the iced fire of your kiss;
only on water my lips, where your face . . .

where your face was reflected, lovely,
not really there when I turned
to look behind at the emptying air . . .

the emptying air.

2011

The Female Husband

Having been, in my youth, a pirate
with cutlass and parrot, a gobful of bad words
yelled at the salty air to curse a cur to the end
of a plank; having jumped ship

in a moonstruck port,
opened an evil bar – a silver coin for a full flask,
a gold coin for don't ask – and boozed and bragged
with losers and hags for a year; having disappeared,

a new lingo's herby zest on my tongue,
to head South on a mule, where a bandit man
took gringo me to the heart of his gang; having robbed
the bank, the coach, the train, the saloon, outdrawn

the sheriff, the deputy sheriff, the deputy's deputy, caught
the knife of an enemy chief in my teeth; having crept
away
from the camp fire, clipped upstream for a night
and a day on a stolen horse,

till I reached the tip
of the century and the lip of the next – it was nix to me
to start again with a new name, a stranger to fame.
Which was how I came to this small farm,

my new wife
on my arm, tattooed on my wrist,
where we have cows and sheep and hens and geese
and keep good bees.

2011

Rings

I might have raised your hand to the sky
to give you the ring surrounding the moon
or looked to twin the rings of your eyes
with mine
                    or added a ring to the rings of a tree
by forming a handheld circle with you, thee,
or walked with you
                              where a ring of church-bells
looped the fields,
or kissed a lipstick ring on your cheek,
a pressed flower,
                          or met with you
in the ring of an hour,
and another hour . . .
                              I might
have opened your palm to the weather, turned, turned,
till your fingers were ringed in rain
or held you close,
                          they were playing our song,
in the ring of a slow dance
or carved our names
in the rough ring of a heart

or heard the ring of an owl's hoot
as we headed home in the dark
or the ring, first thing,
                                        of chorusing birds
waking the house
or given the ring of a boat, rowing the lake,
or the ring of swans, monogamous, two,
or the watery rings made by the fish
as they leaped and splashed
or the ring of the sun's reflection there . . .
I might have tied
                                  a blade of grass,
a green ring for your finger,
or told you the ring of a sonnet by heart
or brought you a lichen ring,
found on a warm wall,
or given a ring of ice in winter
                                                  or in the snow
sung with you the five gold rings of a carol
or stolen a ring of your hair
or whispered the word in your ear
that brought us here,
where nothing and no one is wrong,
and therefore I give you this ring.

2011

Spell

Yes, I think a poem is a spell of kinds
that keeps things living in a written line,
whatever's lost or leaving – lock of rhyme –
and so I write and write and write your name.

2011

New Vows

From this day forth to unhold,
to see the nothing in ringed gold,
uncare for you when you are old.

New vows you make me swear to keep –
not ever wake with you, or sleep,
or your body, with mine, worship;

this empty hand slipped from your glove,
these lips sip never from our loving cup,
I may not cherish, kiss; unhave, unlove . . .

And all my worldly goods to unendow . . .
And who here present upon whom I call . . .

2011

Drone

An upward rush on stairs of air
to the bliss of nowhere, higher,
a living jewel, warm amber, her,
to be the one who would die there.

2011

Chaucer's Valentine

The lyf so short, the craft so long to lerne . . .
but be my valentine
                                        and I'll one candle burn,
love's light a fluent tongue,
old habit young, the door ajar
to where our bed awaits,
                                              not in a room
but in a wood, all thrilled with birds,
the flight of early English words to verse,
there as sweetness evermore now is,
this human kiss,
                                  love's written bliss in every age . . .
hold the front page.

2014

An Unseen

I watched love leave, turn, wave, want not to go,
depart, return;
late spring, a warm slow blue of air, old-new.
Love was here; not; missing, love was there;
each look, first, last.

Down the quiet road, away, away, towards
the dying time,
love went, brave soldier, the song dwindling;
walked to the edge of absence; all moments going,
gone; bells through rain

to fall on the carved names of the lost. I saw
love's child uttered,
unborn, only by rain, then and now, all future
past, an unseen. Has forever been then? Yes,
forever has been.

2014

Stone Love

(for Tracey Emin)

I married a tall, dark, handsome stone
in its lichen suit; secret, sacred, the ceremony
above the sea; where the stone had stood
for a million years, stoic, bridegroom,
till I came at last to the wedding-day.
Gulls laughed in a blue marquee of air.

Shroud for a dress, barefoot, me, my vows
my business and the stone's; but should you ever
press your face to a stone's old, cold, still breast,
you'll find the words which spliced me there
to the silence of stone, till death . . . slow art
of stone, staunchness of stone . . . do us part.

My hand on what I take from time and this world
and the stone's shadow there on the grass with mine.

2018

CXVI

Our two heads on one pillow, I awake
to hear impediments scratch in the room
like rats.
                    I let you sleep, dream on.
                                                            Your face
is summer, cloudless, innocent; it blooms.
My kiss, a dying bee grazing a rose.

Something is wrong.
                                Or let a sonnet prove
the star we followed more than failing light
from time long gone.
                                Love is not love.
Your heart on mine, I feel, a marriage rite –
but on the floor there lie no wedding clothes.

Don't stir.

The curtains won't permit the sun.

Our minds are distant; sullen earth, cold moon

Out of the corner of my eye,

I see them flit,

dark inklings, verminous.

Let me admit . . .

2018

Physics

In the multiple universe theory
                                        of quantum physics
we did get married.
                              For better and for worse,
we are there and there, elsewhere;
                                          not here,
where I stand, solo, free as a spinster,
barefoot on warm grass,
                                  sinking a spritzer,
gleeful . . . *There is a God* . . .
                                      and you
are wherever; beyond care.

But I do wonder
how we are doing,
the flipside of that swithering coin,
after the nuptials,
petals in our hair.
You walk towards me across the terrace,
all I want of love
in that world –
correct when you promised
all would be well. Well,
then again, I feign sleep at your footfall
and we are in Hell.

2018

Roundstone

On the beach at Roundstone,
where my parents' ashes
had separately embarked,
I walked out of love.

I deciphered my mother's advice
from the sea's lisp, its *wheesht*,
as I crossed the line in the sand
some lover had scored through a heart.

And it wasn't a mobile phone
I put to my ear, but a conch;
taking instruction from echoes
to exit the wrong life.

A low sun, nailing its colours to a mast.
My seaweed wreath, left for the tide to accept.

2018

When Then

I knelt in the garden then,
trying to grow a flower from your name;
where blossoms stalled upon their stems,
till you should give permission for the rain.
Hiding in the undergrowth, a wren –
when then was is, I wish my heart had done the same.

2022